Willow Watts and the Green School Wish

Written by
Annie R. Donnelly

Illustrated by
Venessa V. Kelley

Willow Watts and the Green School Wish
Text © 2014 – Annie Donnelly
Illustrations © 2014 - Venessa Kelley
(http://www.RedAdmiralStudio.com)
Printed in United States of America (USA)
Published by Great Books 4 Kids
(http://www.GreatBooks4Kids.org)

ISBN 978-0-9893364-3-7

RA red admiral
CREATIVE STUDIO
www.RedAdmiralStudio.com

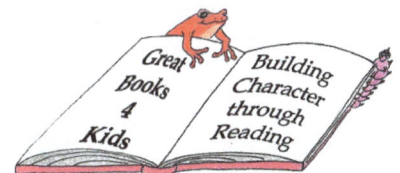

Great Books 4 Kids

Building Character through Reading

I0190646

To my father, who always encouraged me to dream big.

Willow Watts is a curious and smart girl. She loves science, learning new things, her dog Spark and playing outside in her hometown of Greenville.

Like Willow, the people of Greenville love being outside. They ride bikes, run and hike. They make an effort to keep Greenville clean and green. They power their homes and businesses with energy from the sun, wind and water. They conserve energy, they save water and they recycle their garbage.

Greenville is governed by a kind and cheerful queen named Mother Earth. Mother Earth is beautiful just like the land she rules.

Across the ocean from Greenville is Smogville. Smogville is dull. It's a land of brown fields, grey buildings and factories with smokestacks.

The people of Smogville don't spend much time outdoors. They are not active. They do not take care of the environment. They drive cars, trucks and buses that release dirty fumes into the air. They power their homes and businesses with energy from power plants that release dark smoke into the air. They waste energy and water. They don't recycle.

Smogville is ruled by King Smog. King Smog is grumpy and the people of Smogvillle never see him. He sits in his castle all day.

The only thing that brings a smile to King Smog's face is a visit from his granddaughter, Princess Sapphire Smog. She fills the hallways of the dark stone castle with laughter, joy and hope.

"Grandpa Smog, I know what I want for my birthday," said Princess Smog.

"What would you like, my dear?" asked King Smog.

"A new school," said Princess Smog. "I want a green school. A school like Willow Watts's school in Greenville."

"Who is Willow Watts?" asked King Smog.

Dear Princess Smog,
You can make a difference in Smogville by making small changes in your life. Turn off the water while you are brushing your teeth. Always use two sides of a piece of paper before throwing it away. By making these small changes, you can save energy, water, and trees. You can do it, Princess!

Green Dreams!
Willow Watts

"Willow Watts is my pen pal. She lives in Greenville," said Princess Smog. "She writes me letters about life in Greenville and I write her letters about life in Smogville. I've learned so much from Willow Watts."

"Why do you want a new school?" asked King Smog. "You already have a school. What's so special about Willow Watts's school?"

"Smogville Elementary School is so dull," said Princess Smog. "It's an old, dark building. I want to attend a school like Greenville Elementary School. Willow says it's clean, bright, colorful and cheerful. They have a garden, a playground and lights that turn on when you walk in the classroom and turn off when you walk out of the classroom. It sounds magical!"

"School is a place for learning, Princess," said King Smog. "It's not a place for magic."

"You don't understand Grandpa," said Princess Smog. "You haven't visited Smogville Elementary School since you were a boy. The building is falling apart."

"Please come to school with me tomorrow Grandpa," said Princess Smog. "I will show you why I want a new school for my birthday. It would be a present for me, and one I can share with the students and teachers."

"Alright Princess," said King Smog. "I'll visit Smogville Elementary School with you tomorrow."

The next day King Smog and Princess Smog arrived at Smogville Elementary School. The old concrete building had seen better days.

"Good Morning King Smog," said Principal Drought. "Welcome Back to Smogville Elementary School."

"Thank you, Principal Drought," said King Smog. "It's been a long time. You have not done much with the building since I was a student here."

"No sir," said Principal Drought. "We know you don't like change."

Principal Drought led King Smog and Princess Smog down the hallway.

"Look at the floor. It's cracked. The paint on the wall is peeling. The lockers are broken," said Princess Smog. "And that water fountain, has been leaking, since I was in kindergarten. It's been forever!"

"I see Princess," said King Smog. "This is terrible. This is not how I remembered Smogville Elementary School."

King Smog, Princess Smog and Principal Drought entered Ms. Dusty's science classroom. "I can't hear what she is saying," said King Smog. "All I can hear is the traffic and noise coming from outside, it's very distracting."

"I know Grandpa," said Princess Smog. "I told Willow Watts about this in one of my letters. She calls it noise pollution. Willow says that the walls in the classrooms at her school are so strong, they block noise from the outside."

Aa Bb Cc Dd Ee Ff Gg Hh Ii

"It's hard to see the writing on the chalkboard," said King Smog. "This classroom is so dark. I can only read the writing on the chalkboard if I'm standing right in front of it. How can you learn anything in a loud, dark classroom?" asked King Smog.

"I'm not learning very much," said Princess Smog. "I'm so distracted by the noise that I can't focus. It makes me sad because science is my favorite subject."

"What class is this?" asked King Smog.

"This is gym class," said Princess Smog. "Coach Sloth taught us all how to play a card game."

"This is ridiculous," said King Smog. "This is not a gym class! When I was a boy, we learned how to play sports. We played basketball, volleyball and soccer. We ran around and stretched our legs. We didn't sit in silence and play cards."

"Coach Sloth," said King Smog, "Why aren't you teaching the students a sport? Why aren't they outside on the playground?"

"Sir, all our equipment is so old. It needs to replaced," replied Coach Sloth. "It's not safe for our students to play in this gym or outside in the schoolyard. They could get hurt."

King Smog looked outside at the playground and couldn't believe his eyes. He had loved gym class as a boy, but as he looked around he saw the schoolyard overgrown with weeds, a ripped soccer net and garbage thrown on the field.

"This is so sad," said King Smog.

SMOGVILLE FEILD *Home of* THE SMOKESTACKS!

Following their visit to the school gym, King Smog and Princess Smog headed to the cafeteria for lunch.

"I hope you're not very hungry Grandpa," whispered Princess Smog. "The cafeteria food isn't very good."

"How do you eat this food?" asked King Smog.

"I don't," said Princess Smog. "I throw it away."

"That's so wasteful," said King Smog."

"I'm not the only one Grandpa," said Princess Smog. "All my classmates throw their lunch away. Look at the garbage can."

TRASH

King Smog returned to his castle, saddened by what he saw at Smogville Elementary School. It was not a healthy or safe place for children to learn. Perhaps, it was time to visit Greenville, meet Willow Watts and tour her school. He picked up the phone to call Mother Earth.

"Hello, Mother Earth. This is King Smog of Smogville," said King Smog.

"King Smog, what a surprise! I have not heard from you in years," said Mother Earth. "How can I help you?"

"My granddaughter Princess Smog has heard wonderful things about Greenvlle Elementary School from a student named Willow Watts," said King Smog. "Have you heard of this girl?"

"Yes, of course," said Mother Earth. "Willow Watts is one of Greenville Elementary School's brightest students."

"Can you please arrange for Willow Watts to give my granddaughter and I a tour of the school tomorrow?" asked King Smog.

"I would be happy to arrange a tour for you and Princess Smog," said Mother Earth. "Willow will make an excellent tour guide."

The following day, King Smog and Princess Smog arrived at Greenvile Elementary School and were greeted by Willow Watts, her dog Spark and Principal Sunny. "Welcome to Greenville," said Willow. "We're so happy to have you here today!"

Greenville
Elementa

DON'T MISS T
GREEN FESTIVA

Willow led King Smog
and Princess Smog into the lobby
of Greenville Elementary School.

"Wow," said Princess Smog. "It's so
bright in here. A big difference from the dark
lobby of Smogville Elementary School."

"The large windows allow the sun to shine into the
lobby," said Willow Watts. "The sunlight heats and lights our lobby."

Princess Smog looked down at the floor. "This floor looks so pretty in the sunlight," said Princess Smog. "It looks like it's made of colorful crystals."

"This floor is made of recycled glass," said Willow Watts.

"Recycled glass?" asked Princess Smog.

"Yes," said Willow Watts. "This floor is a jigsaw puzzle of pieces of glass that were once part of a flower vase, a tea cup and a window."

"It's beautiful," said Princess Smog.

"What's that?" asked Princess Smog. "Is that a time machine?!"

"No, Princess Smog. It's an elevator," said Willow Watts. "Instead of bringing people back in time, it carries people from the first floor to the second floor. Come on, let's take a ride to the second floor."

Willow led Princess Smog and King Smog onto the elevator. "This is a very special elevator," said Willow Watts. "It's energy efficient."

"What does that mean?" asked King Smog.

"It uses energy in a useful way," said Willow Watts. "As it moves up and down between the floors, it saves and reuses energy again and again."

Willow Watts, King Smog and Princess Smog entered Ms. Clean's science class.

"Welcome," said Ms. Clean. "Please take a seat."

Ms. Clean continued her lesson as King Smog, Princess Smog and Willow sat at one of the lab stations in the back of the classroom.

King Smog raised his hand. "King Smog, do you have a question?" asked Ms. Clean.

"Yes," said King Smog. "What makes the air in this room so clean?"

"There are several reasons," said Ms. Clean. "Willow, can you please answer King Smog's question?"

"Of course! The air in this classroom is clean because the floor, the paint on the walls, the lab tables and chairs are all made from clean materials," said Willow. "They are non-toxic. Free from chemicals. Chemicals can make the air dirty and make people sick."

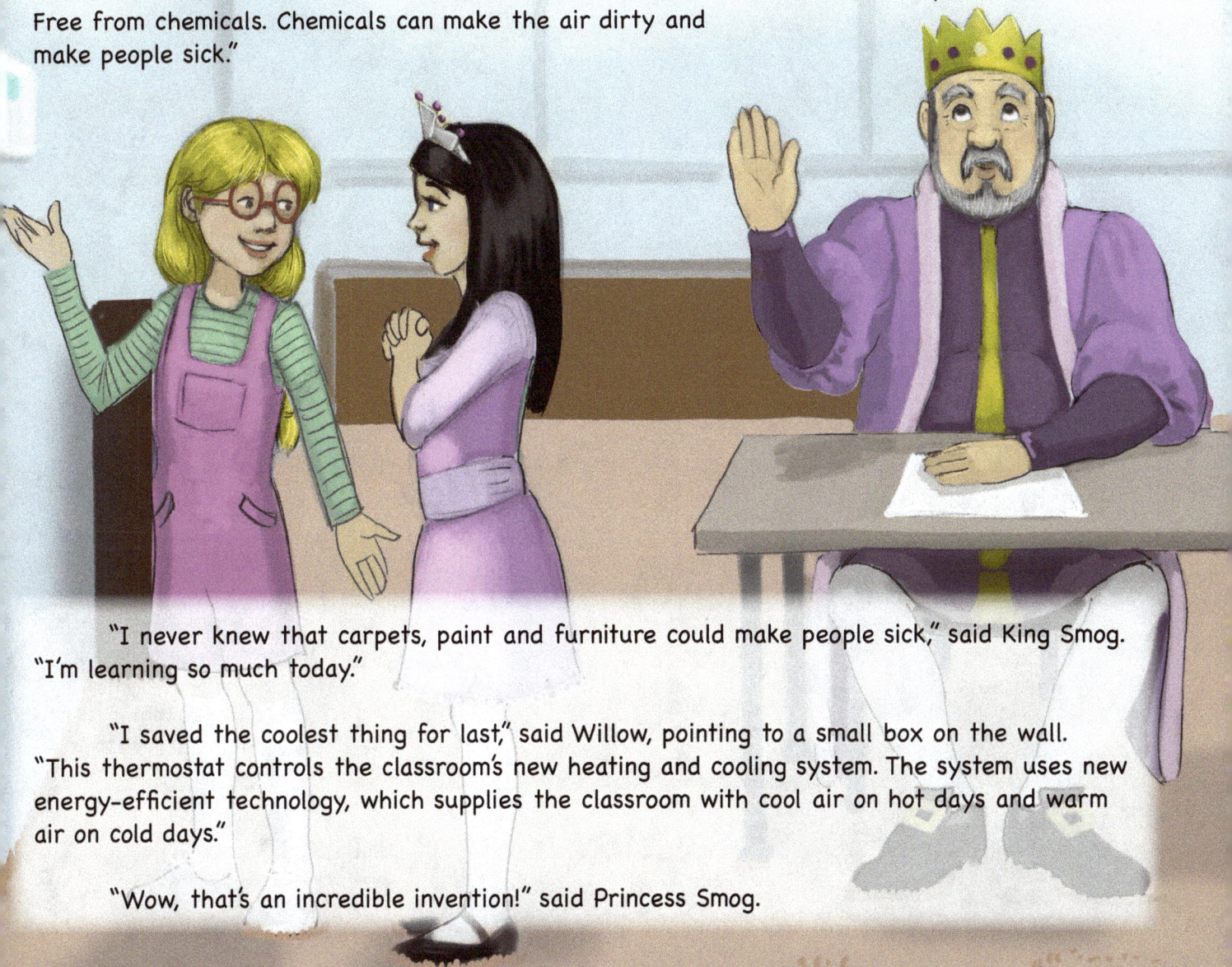

"I never knew that carpets, paint and furniture could make people sick," said King Smog. "I'm learning so much today."

"I saved the coolest thing for last," said Willow, pointing to a small box on the wall. "This thermostat controls the classroom's new heating and cooling system. The system uses new energy-efficient technology, which supplies the classroom with cool air on hot days and warm air on cold days."

"Wow, that's an incredible invention!" said Princess Smog.

Departing Miss Clean's classroom, King Smog, Princess Smog and Willow Watts changed their clothes and headed to gym class with Coach Fit.

"Are you enjoying your tour of Greenville School?" asked Coach Fit.

"Yes," said Princess Smog. "I'm having a wonderful day."

"How about you King Smog?" asked Coach Fit. "Are you having fun?"

"I'm learning a lot and feeling full of energy," said King Smog.

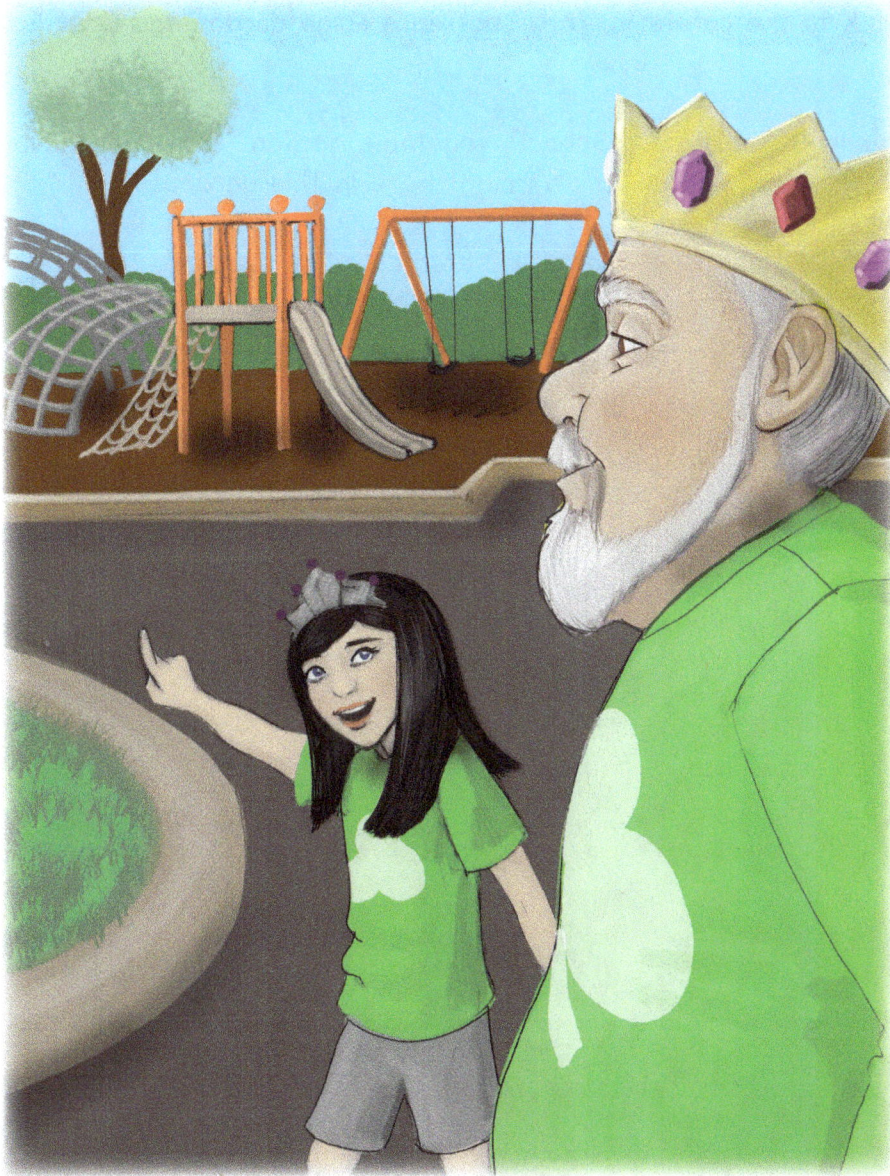

"This school yard is amazing!" said Princess Smog. "My friends in Smogville will never believe it when I tell them about this place. It's like a fairy tale."

"It's wonderful," said King Smog. "This is what a schoolyard should look like."

After gym class, Willow Watts, King Smog and Princess Smog changed out of their gym clothes and headed toward the school cafeteria.

On their walk to the cafeteria, they spotted a large garden and Chef Flavor, who was harvesting plants.

"This is Greenville Elementary School's vegetable garden," said Chef Flavor. "All the vegetables in our school lunches are grown right here in this garden."

"I have never seen so many colorful vegetables in my life," said Princess Smog. "Our school lunches don't include any of these beautiful colored vegetables."

Chef Flavor led Willow Watts and Princess Smog to the cafeteria as King Smog departed to a lunch meeting in Principal Sunny's office. "I have a rule in my cafeteria," said Chef Flavor. "Everyone must have at least four colors on their plate. I believe variety is the spice of life!"

Following Chef Flavor's instructions, they filled their lunch plates with a variety of vegetables from the school garden.

"This lunch is so much better than Chef Bland's lunch," said Princess Smog. Looking around the cafeteria, Princess Smog then noticed three blue bins in the corner. The bins had symbols on them. "What are those bins for, Willow?," asked Princess Smog.

"We recycle," said Willow Watts.

Landfill   Paper   Plastic

After lunch, Willow and Princess Smog met King Smog on the way to math class with Mr. Addition.

"I will not be joining you in math class," said King Smog. "I must attend a meeting with Mother Earth, but Princess Smog can stay for the rest of the school day."

"Thank you, Grandpa!" said Princess Smog. "I don't want this day to end. I wish my friends from Smogville Elementary School could be here to enjoy it too. They would love Greenville Elementary School."

King Smog was very impressed with Greenville Elementary School. The students and teachers were so cheerful and happy. They took pride in their school. It was nothing like the dreary sadness that filled the halls and classrooms of Smogville Elementary School. King Smog knew that he had to make a change, but he didn't know where to begin, he needed Mother Earth's help.

Months later, Princess Smog's birthday had finally arrived. That morning, King Smog entered her room and handed her a small box. "Happy Birthday!" said King Smog. "I hope you like it."

Princess Smog's heart sank. All she wanted for her birthday was a green school. A green school could not fit in a small box.

Princess Smog unwrapped the paper and opened the box. "A key?" asked Princess Smog, looking up at her grandfather, "Does it open something?"

King Smog nodded his head and said, "Follow me."

After a short trip from Smogville castle, King Smog and Princess Smog arrived in front of a new building, a building Princess Smog had never seen before.

"Is this a dream?" asked Princess Smog. "What is this building doing in Smogville?"

King Smog laughed. "No, my dear. You are not dreaming. That building is real and the key you are holding opens the front door. Go ahead. Open the front door!"

SMOGVILLE
ELEMENTARY SCHOOL

Princess Smog opened the door. The hallway was lined with shiny blue lockers, the white tile floor sparkled in the sunlight pouring in from the skylights in the ceiling. Before Princess Smog, stood a crowd of people from Smogville and Greenville, including Willow Watts, who held a cupcake.

"Surprise!!" shouted the crowd.

"Welcome to the new Smogville Elementary School, where birthday wishes and dreams come true!" said Willow Watts. "Make a wish!"

That day, Princess Smog made a new wish for King Smog to govern Smogville with a green thumb. Thanks to Willow Watts, Mother Earth and the teachers of Greenville Elementary School, that is exactly what he did.

The End

King Smog's Green School Building Checklist

- ☑ Hire Mother's Earth's Green Team of engineers, builders and landscape designers

- ☑ Solar panels for roof of school

- ☑ Skylights and large windows

- ☑ Recycled building materials including concrete wood and glass

- ☑ Furnish classrooms with furniture made from clean materials

- ☑ Include insulation in walls to block noise from outside

- ☑ Use non-toxic paint for walls

- ☑ Water saving fountains and sinks

- ☑ Plant a vegetable garden

- ☑ Build a new schoolyard with a safe playground

- ☑ Install an energy efficient elevator and heating and cooling system

- ☑ Add recycle bins to all classrooms and cafeteria

- ☑ Invite Willow Watts to teach students about the green features of their new school

- ☑ Make this the school of Princess Smog's dreams

www.ingramcontent.com/pod-product-compliance
Lightning Source LLC
Chambersburg PA
CBHW081232020426
42331CB00012B/3142